Livewires

STARTER

OXFORD UNIVERSITY PRESS 1998

Kate Wakeman • • • • • • • • **Danae Kozanoglou**

Contents

unit	story	learning objectives	language focus
9	Iceman!	• expressing abilities • talking about different activities • giving instructions	• *can/can't* to express ability • imperatives
10	Fast food	• ordering food in a restaurant • discussing prices • expressing strong likes and dislikes	• countable and uncountable nouns • *some* and *any* • questions with *How many ...?*
REVISION	Units 6–10		
11	New York	• asking about and describing actions in progress • miming	• present continuous tense • spelling rules with the *-ing* ending
12	The escape	• learning about people from other countries • talking about where you live	• present simple tense: *live* • countries and nationalities • animals
13	The rainforest	• describing people • describing animals	• animals • parts of the body • adjectives used to describe people
14	The end of Iceman	• predicting the future • expressing intention • talking about the weather and holiday activities	• days of the week • the *going to* future • the weather and seasons
15	The storm	• talking about daily/weekly routines	• present simple tense for routines • prepositions *on, at, in* with times and days
REVISION	Units 11–15		
GRAMMAR SUMMARY			

Meet the Livewires

● What's this?

1 Ask and answer with your teacher.

2 Point, ask and answer.

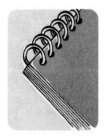  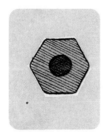

1   2   3

  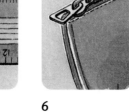

4   5   6

3 Draw six things. Ask your teacher for words you need. Point, ask and answer again.

1   2   3

4   5   6

Look!

What's ...? = What is ...?

It's ... = It is ...

1 ❶ Listen and read.
2 Match the letters.
3 Now sing the song.

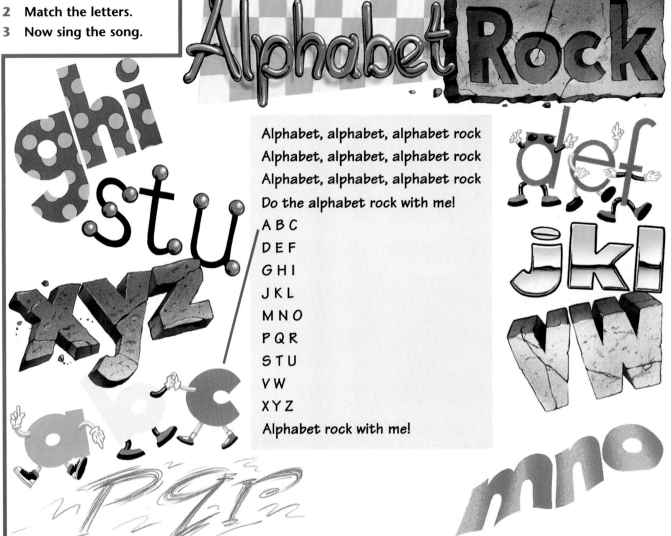

Alphabet Rock

Alphabet, alphabet, alphabet rock
Alphabet, alphabet, alphabet rock
Alphabet, alphabet, alphabet rock
Do the alphabet rock with me!
A B C
D E F
G H I
J K L
M N O
P Q R
S T U
V W
X Y Z
Alphabet rock with me!

● How do you spell ...?

1 ❷ Listen and repeat.
2 Ask and answer with your teacher.
3 Ask and answer with your friend.

4 Spelling game. Play in groups

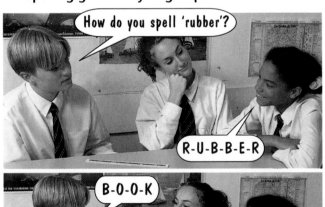

How are you?

1  ❸ Listen and repeat.
2 Practise the dialogue.

Look!

I'm = I am

thanks = thank you

Hi! I'm Watt.

Think about it!

1 **What's this?**

1 It's a pencil. 2 .... 3 ....

4 .... 5 ....

2 **Match the names and faces.**

Sparks   Flick   Martin   Kim

(a) (b) (c) (d)

3 **Complete the speech bubbles.**

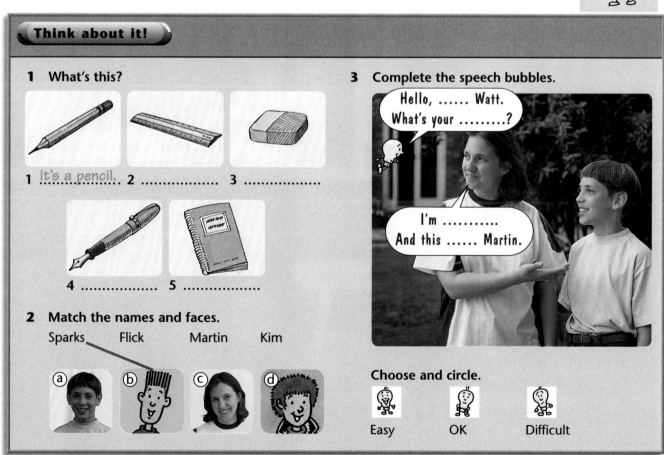

Hello, ... Watt.
What's your ....?

I'm ....
And this ...... Martin.

Choose and circle.

Easy   OK   Difficult

Where's Buzz?

Prepositions

1 **Where's Watt? Match the pictures and sentences.**

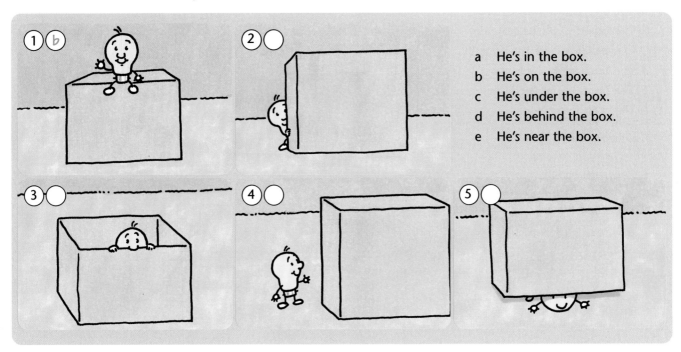

a He's in the box.
b He's on the box.
c He's under the box.
d He's behind the box.
e He's near the box.

2 **Look at the picture. Match.**

Buzz is ———— behind the car.
Sparks is near the tree.
Watt is in the garage.
Dazzle is on the car.

3 **Who is under the car?**

.... *is under the car.*

Look!

he =   she =

4 Listen and repeat.
5 Listen and answer.
6 Draw yourself in the picture. Say where you are.
I'm ...

In the classroom

1 🎞 ❸ **Listen and repeat.**

1 The girl is behind the door.
2 The board is on the wall.
3 The pencil is near the book.
4 The book is on the table.
5 The bin is under the table.
6 The ruler is in the bin.

2 **Ask and answer.**

Where's the pencil?
It's near the book.
Where's the girl?
She's behind the door.

3 🎞 ❹ **Listen. Write the letters on the picture.**

4 Draw the things on the picture.

5 Choose something. Your friend guesses.

Is it on the wall?
No, it isn't.
Is it on the table?
Yes, it is.
Is it the bin?
Yes, it is.

6 Add a pen, a book, and a rubber to the picture. Then ask and answer.

Where's the pen?
It's under the pencil case.

The Watt Rap

1  ⑤ Listen and point.
2 Say the rap.

Where's Watt?
He's on the floor.
Where's Watt?
Behind the door.
Where's Watt?
There! There!
Under the table!
Under the chair!

Think about it!

1 Complete the sentences.

Sparks is ...... the car. Buzz is .... the wall.
Watt is .... the car. Dazzle is .... the
wall.

2 Match.

table   tree   garage   door

3 Complete the speech bubbles.

.... my bag?

It's ....
the ....

Choose and circle.

Easy   OK   Difficult

X-ray vision

☾ In the shed ...

1 Match the words and pictures.

poster   ⑥

cushion   ☐

blanket   ☐

box   ☐

book   ☐

chair   ☐

torch   ☐

TV   ☐

umbrella   ☐

aeroplane   ☐

bin   ☐

phone   ☐

2 ▭ ❶ Listen and repeat.

3 ▭ ❷ Listen and match.

4 ▭ ❸ Listen. Draw Sparks' bedroom.

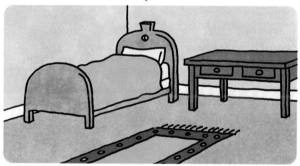

5 Draw your bedroom. Describe it.

In my bedroom, there's ...

6 Choose a bedroom. Your friend guesses.

Is there a table?
Yes, there is.
Is there a poster?
No, there isn't.
Is it Buzz's bedroom?
Yes, it is!

Look!

| a book | an umbrella |
| a torch | an aeroplane |

X-ray vision

1 Take a piece of paper. Draw the inside of a cupboard.

2 Draw four things in the cupboard. Don't show your friend.

3 Turn the piece of paper over.

4 Trace the lines and draw the doors.

5 Ask and answer.

6 Now use your x-ray vision and check.

Let's do it!

1 Listen and point.
2  Say the chant.

Go to the window!
No, no, no!
Open the door!
No, no, no!
Jump up and down!
Yes, let's do it!
Let's all jump up and down!

Open your book!
No, no, no!
Do your homework!
No, no, no!
Turn around!
Yes, let's do it!
Let's all turn around!

Think about it!

1 What's on the table?

1 There's a ....
2 ....
3 ....
4 ....
5 ....

2 Match.

draw   write   sing   listen

3 Complete the speech bubbles.

.... there a TV in the shed?

Yes, there .... It's .... the table.

Choose and circle.

Easy   OK   Difficult

Into the book

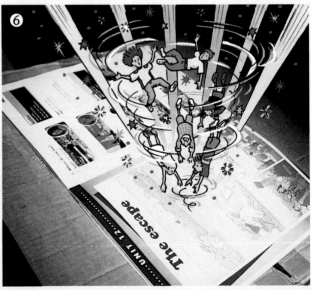

Numbers

1 ① **Listen and point. Then say the numbers.**

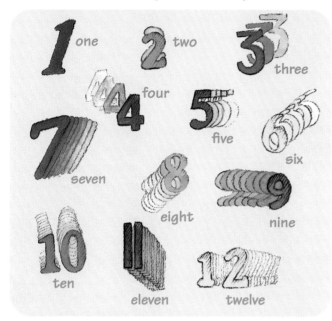

one two three
four five six
seven eight nine
ten eleven twelve

2 ② **Listen. Join the numbers in the order you hear them. What is the picture?**

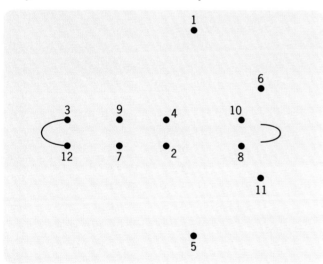

How old are you?

1 ③ **Listen and repeat.**

SCAT
SPLAT
SMAT
BRAT
I'm one!
I'm three!
I'm five!
How old are you?

2 **Ask and answer.**

How old are you?
I'm ....

3 ④ **Listen and repeat.**

13 thirteen   17 seventeen
14 fourteen   18 eighteen
15 fifteen   19 nineteen
16 sixteen   20 twenty

4 ⑤ **Listen and point to the people.**

03:57 pm

03:59 pm

04:02 pm

5 **Bring photos. Talk about your family.**

This is my brother. He's sixteen. His name's …

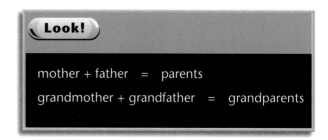

Look!

mother + father = parents

grandmother + grandfather = grandparents

Where are you from?

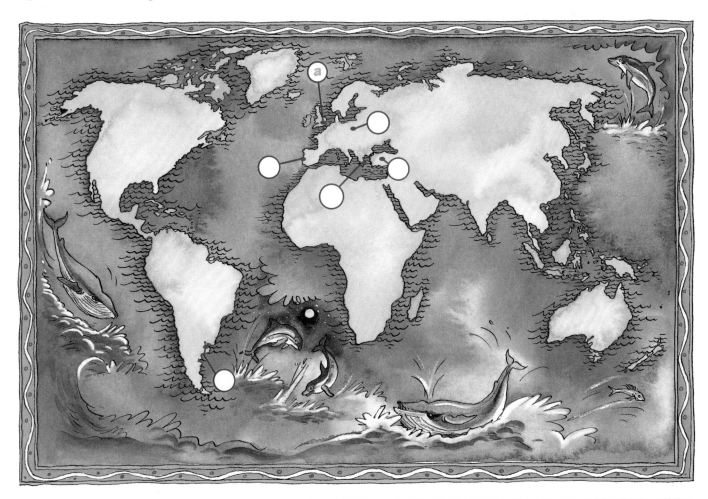

Capital cities

a London ...England......   d Lisbon ....

b Athens ....   e Ankara ....

c Buenos Aires ....   f Warsaw ....

Countries

Turkey   Portugal

Greece   England

Argentina   Poland

1 Label the cities.

2 Match the cities and the countries.

3 🔊 **6** Listen and check your answers.

4 Add more cities and countries to the map.

5 Choose a city. Ask and answer.

Where are you from?
I'm from London.
Where's that?
It's in England.

6 Choose a country. Your friend guesses.

Are you from Argentina?
No, I'm not.
Are you from Poland?
Yes, I am!

7 🔊 **7** Listen. Complete the information.

Departures ✈		
Flight number	**Destination**	**Gate**
AZ 717	Rome	....
BA 631	....	7
TK 848	Istanbul	....
TW 881	....	2
SU 296	Moscow	....

Shooting Stars!

1 🎹 ⑧ **Listen and point.**

2 **Listen again. Complete the information.**

3 **Work in groups. Act out the interviews.**

Number	1	2	3	4
Name	Sophie			Tina
From		Portugal		
Age			13	

Think about it!

1 **Write four cities and countries.**

Cities   Countries

.... is in ....

.... is in ....

.... is in ....

.... is in ....

2 **Write these numbers in words.**

11 ....

2 ....

8 ....

19 ....

7 ....

3 ....

3 **Draw yourself in the picture. Complete the speech bubbles.**

My .... Martin.
I'm .... England.
Where .... you from?

I'm ....
....

Choose and circle.

Easy   OK   Difficult

The Livewires Express

● Colours

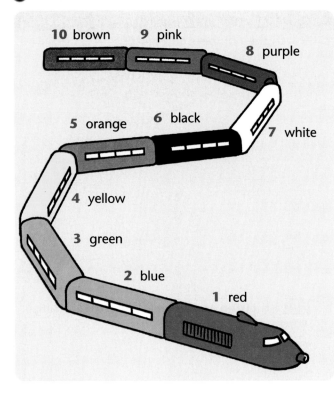

```
10 brown    9 pink
                    8 purple
    5 orange   6 black
                         7 white
        4 yellow
        3 green
            2 blue
                    1 red
```

1 📻 ❶ Listen and repeat.
2 Find these things in your classroom. What colour are they?

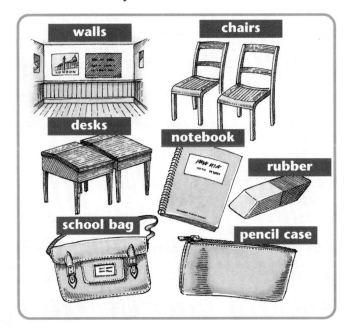

walls   chairs
desks   notebook
         rubber
school bag   pencil case

The board is black.

The desks are brown.

● Plurals and numbers

1 Find, count and match.
2 📻 ❷ Listen and check your answers.

videos	2
books	3
rubbers	4
cushions	5
bats	6
candles	7
chairs	8
boxes	9

Pronunciation

3 📻 ❸ Look at the words in Exercise 2. Listen and repeat.

4 Listen again. Write the words in the correct box.

/s/	/z/	/ɪz/

5 📻 ❹ Listen and repeat. Then ask and answer about the other things.

How many books are there?
There are eight.
What colour are they?
They're green.

Look!

one person   two people

What's in the box?

1 Look and say.

There are six pencils.

There's a school bag.

2 🔊 **5** What's in the cupboard? Listen and draw.

3 Colour the objects in your picture.

4 Write a list.

Number	Colour	Object
1	green	ruler
3	blue	pencils

5 Ask and answer about your friend's picture.

What colour is the ruler?

It's green.

What colour are the pencils?

They're blue.

Numbers 20–100

1 🔊 **6** Listen and repeat.

2 Match the numbers and words.

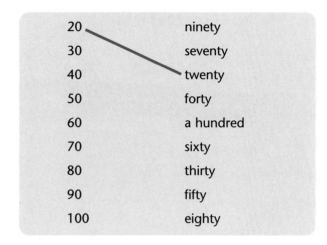

20	ninety
30	seventy
40	twenty
50	forty
60	a hundred
70	sixty
80	thirty
90	fifty
100	eighty

3 🔊 **7** Listen and repeat. Write the missing words.

21 twenty-one

22 twenty-two

23 ....-three

24 twenty-..................

25 ....-..................

26 ....-..................

27 ....-..................

28 ....-..................

29 ....-..................

30 ....

4 Choose six of the numbers and write one in each box.

5 🔊 **8** Play bingo! Listen and tick (✔) the numbers.

Kim's family tree

1 Look at Kim's family tree.

Hannah, my grandmother
Age 71

Stuart, my grandfather
Age 74

Ann, my aunt
Age 35

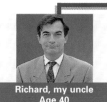

Richard, my uncle
Age 40

Rod, my father
Age 39

Lynn, my mother
Age 37

Me!
Age 12

Martin, my brother
Age 11

2 Complete the dialogue between Kim and her friend Julie.

Kim Look! This is a picture of my (1) ....

Julie How (2) .... is he?

Kim He's eleven.

Julie Is that your (3)................?

Kim Yes, it is. Her (4).............. is Lynn.

Julie And this is your (5) ....

Kim No, it (6) ....! It's his brother, Richard. He's my (7) ....

Julie Who's this?

Kim My (8) .... He's 74!

3 🔊 ⑨ **Listen and check your answers.**

4 **Ask and answer about the people in Kim's family tree.**

How old is Kim's aunt?
She's 35.
What's her name?
Her name's Ann.

Think about it!

1 Read and colour.
There are two blue candles, three yellow candles and five red candles.

2 Write the words.

43 ....

21 ....

70 ....

84 ....

3 Write the numbers.

a hundred ....

sixty-eight ....

thirty-three ....

fifty-nine ....

4 Write the plurals.

bat ....

box ....

person ....

video ....

Choose and circle.

Easy   OK   Difficult

Revision

Units 1-5

Stop and think!

- Do the exercises on pages 24–26. Start with 'Countries of the world'.
- Look at the HELP screens if you need more practice.

A	Countries of the world	OK	HELP
B	Families	OK	HELP
C	Numbers, colours and prepositions	OK	HELP
D	The verb 'be'	OK	HELP
E	Questions	OK	HELP

- Colour each letter when you can do the section.

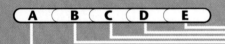

A B C D E

Well done!

A

- Look at the map on page 18 of the Student's Book.
- Use an atlas or a geography book.
- Do Buzz words in Unit 4 of the Workbook.

B

- Look at Kim's family tree on page 23 of the Student's Book.
- Look at the 'Family' page in your vocabulary book.
- Read item 7 of the Grammar Summary.

C

- Look at the colours on page 21 of the Student's Book.
- Learn the prepositions on page 9 of the Student's Book.
- Look at the photograph on page 13 of the Student's Book.

D

- Look at the Look! boxes on pages 5 and 7 of the Student's Book.
- Do Exercises 8 and 9 in Unit 2 of the Workbook.
- Read item 1 of the Grammar Summary.

E

- Look at the story pages in Units 1–5 of the Student's Book.
- Do Exercise 1 in Units 1–5 of the Workbook.
- Read item 1 of the Grammar Summary.

Countries of the world

1 Name this country. Use the map on page 18 to help you.

2 What is its capital city? Label it.

3 Draw more countries in your notebook. Can your friend name the countries and their capitals?

Families

1 **Use these words to complete the table of family members. What are they in your own language?**

sister   niece   uncle   son   grandson
grandfather   mother

♀	♂
grandmother	....
....	father
aunt	....
wife	husband
....	brother
cousin	cousin
daughter	....
....	nephew
granddaughter	....

Look!

my brother's bedroom   my brothers' bedroom

2 **Look at the family tree and solve the puzzles.**

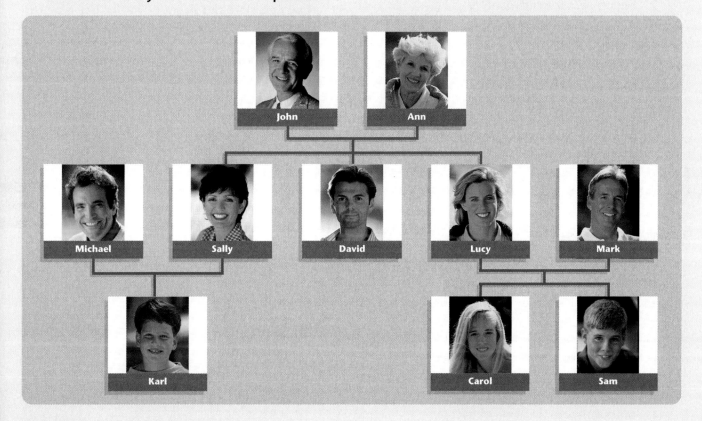

John   Ann

Michael   Sally   David   Lucy   Mark

Karl   Carol   Sam

Puzzles

Who am I?

1 My sisters' names are Sally and Lucy. ....David....
2 My cousin's name is Karl. My sister's name is Carol.
   ....
3 My daughter's name is Sally. My husband's name is John. ....
4 My brother's name is David. My nephew's name is Karl. ....

5 My grandmother's name is Ann. My father's name is Michael. ....
6 My niece's name is Carol. My nephews' names are Karl and Sam. ....

3 **In your notebook, draw your own family tree. Write puzzles for your friend to solve.**

25

Numbers, colours and prepositions

1 Look at the picture and answer the questions.

1 What's in the cupboard?

There are six books. There's a …

2 What's on the bed?

3 What's near the cupboard?

4 What's under the bed?

2 How many things are there in the bedroom? What colour are they?

There are two red books and four green books. There's …

3 Don't look at the picture. Try and answer your friend's questions.

How many books are there?
Six.
That's right!

The verb *be*

1 Look at the table and write the missing words. Use the correct colours.

■ = pronoun   (I, you, he, she, it, we, they)
■ = verb   (am, is, are)

short form	full form
I'm	I am
you're	you ....
he's	he ....
she's	.... is
it's	it ....
we're	.... are
you're	you ....
they're	.... are

2 Complete this text. Use verbs and pronouns from the table in Exercise 1.

This .... my brother, Stuart. .... is fourteen years old. Judy and Emma .... my sisters. .... are ten and sixteen. (Judy .... ten and Emma .... sixteen.) And .... am Rob. I .... twelve.

3 Now complete the negative forms. Use blue for the pronoun and red for the verb.

short form	full form
I'm **not**	I am **not**
.... aren't	you .... **not**
.... isn't	he .... **not**
she	.... is **not**
.... isn't	it .... **not**
we	.... are **not**
you	you .... **not**
they	.... are **not**

Questions

1 Match the questions and answers.

questions	answers
How old is she?	No, she isn't.
What's that?	She's fifteen.
What colour are they?	She's from Egypt.
Where's my book?	They're blue.
Where is she from?	It's under the desk.
Is she your sister?	It's a notebook.

2 What do you notice about the order of the pronoun and verb in questions and answers?

3 How do you make questions in your own language?

Reading and writing

1 Look at the picture. Is this classroom like yours?

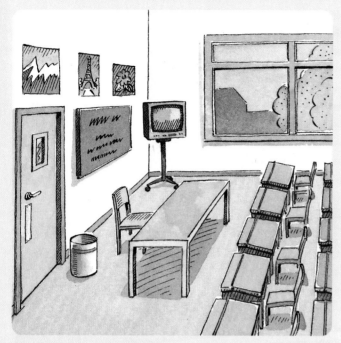

Project idea

- In groups, agree on your ideal classroom.
- Write a description and draw a picture.
- Display your pictures and texts on the wall or in a class book.

2 Read and complete the text. Use these words.

are   TV   chairs   three   chair   door

This is our classroom. There are desks and
(1)............ for the students and a table for the
teacher. The teacher's (2)............ is near the
board. The walls (3)............ white. There are
(4)............ pictures on the wall. There is a bin
near the (5)............ and a (6)............ near
the window.

3 Think of your ideal classroom. Make notes.

There is ...   *a computer*
                  a TV
                  a video recorder
There are...   *lots of books*
                  lots of videos

4 Write a description of your ideal classroom. Use your notes from Exercise 3.

In my classroom, there is ...

Sparks' house

What have they got?

1 🎵 ❶ Listen and point to the things.
2 Listen and repeat.

①
hat
mirror
book
hairbrush
recorder

②
tambourine
basketball
whistle
yo-yo

3 🎵 ❷ Listen and repeat. Match.

scarf ☐
tennis racket ☐
baseball bat ☐
guitar ☐

4 **What has Flick got?**
Flick's got a scarf.
She's got …

5 **Look at page 28 again. What has Sparks got?**
Sparks has got a swimming pool.
He's got …

6 **What have Kim and Martin got?**
Kim and Martin have got a torch.
They've got …

Pronunciation

7 🎵 ❸ Listen and repeat.
a 'book
got a 'book
'Dazzle's got a 'book

a 'whistle
got a 'whistle
'Buzz has got a 'whistle

8 **Make up more.**

Look!

He's got	=	He has got
She's got	=	She has got
They've got	=	They have got

A memory game

1 🔊 ④ **Listen and read. Then read and say.**

I've got...	Your friend (✔ or ✗)
....	☐
....	☐
....	☐
....	☐
....	☐
....	☐

Look!

Dazzle has got a mirror.

Has Dazzle got a mirror?

2 **Ask and answer about Buzz, Flick and Sparks.**

Has Sparks got a ...?
Yes, he has.
Has he got a ...?
No he hasn't.

3 **Ask and answer about Kim and Martin.**

Have Kim and Martin got a ...?
Yes, they have.
Have they got a ...?
No, they haven't.

4 **What have you got? Write six things.**

5 **Ask your friend. Add a tick (✔) or a cross (✗) for each thing.**

Have you got ...?
Yes, I have. (✔) / No, I haven't. (✗)

6 **Talk about you and your friend.**

I've got ...
My friend's got ...
We've both got ...

Look!

I've got = I have got

We've got = We have got

Tock tick tock tick tock tick tock
What's the time on the backward clock?
It's 12 o'clock. Just wait one hour
For 11 o'clock on the big clock tower.

Tock tick tock tick tock tick tock
What's the time on the backward clock?
It's 11 o'clock. Just wait one hour
For 10 o'clock on the big clock tower.

The Backward Clock

Think about it!

1 Label these things.

1 .... 2 ....

3 .... 4 ....

2 Draw and label two more things.

1 .... 2 ....

3 What have they got? Complete the sentences.

Sparks has ...... a swimming pool.
Dazzle .... a hairbrush.
Martin and Kim .... a TV.
I ....

4 What's the time?

1 .... 2 ....

3 .... 4 ....

Choose and circle.

Easy   OK   Difficult

Ms Brush

I want ...

1 Read the story again and answer the questions.

a What does Sparks want?
He wants …

b What does Dazzle want?
She wants …
She doesn't want …

> **Look!**
>
> I want an ice cream.
> He / She wants an ice cream.
> I don't want a sandwich.
> He / She doesn't want a sandwich.

Can I have ...?

1 Complete the speech bubbles.

2 Listen and check your answers.

3 Act out the dialogue.

4 Be Ms Brush! Listen and draw things for Kim and Martin.

5 Answer the questions.

a What does Martin want?

b What does Kim want?

Pronunciation

6 Listen and read the dialogue.

Can I have a piano, please?
OK. Here you are.

7 Listen and repeat. Then make up dialogues for these things.

Do you want …?

1  4 Listen and point.

2 Match. Then listen and repeat.

aeroplane 10
bottle of Coke
car
cassette player
dinosaur
doll
football
guitar
hamburger
motorbike
piano
sandwich
skateboard
television
train
video

3 5 Listen and complete.

4 Listen and repeat.

5 Work in groups of four. Make the cards from Exercises 1 and 2.

6 Choose three things you want and write them in your notebook. Don't tell your friends!

7 Now play the game.

● Reading and writing

1 Complete the letter.

Dear Mum and Dad,

It's my birthday soon. Can I have a  ...., please? A friend at school has got one and it's great! I also want a .... Can I have a .... one please? Thank you very much.

Love, Martin.

2 Make a list of things you want for your birthday.

3 Write a letter.

Dear _____,

Thank you very much,
Love,

Think about it!

1 Look at the pictures.

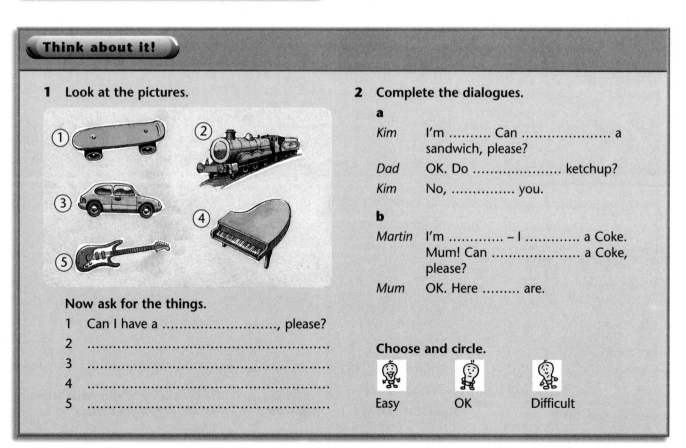

Now ask for the things.
1 Can I have a ...., please?
2 ....
3 ....
4 ....
5 ....

2 Complete the dialogues.

a

Kim   I'm .... Can .... a sandwich, please?

Dad   OK. Do .... ketchup?

Kim   No, ... you.

b

Martin   I'm .... – I .... a Coke. Mum! Can .... a Coke, please?

Mum   OK. Here .... are.

Choose and circle.

Easy   OK   Difficult

Flick's birthday

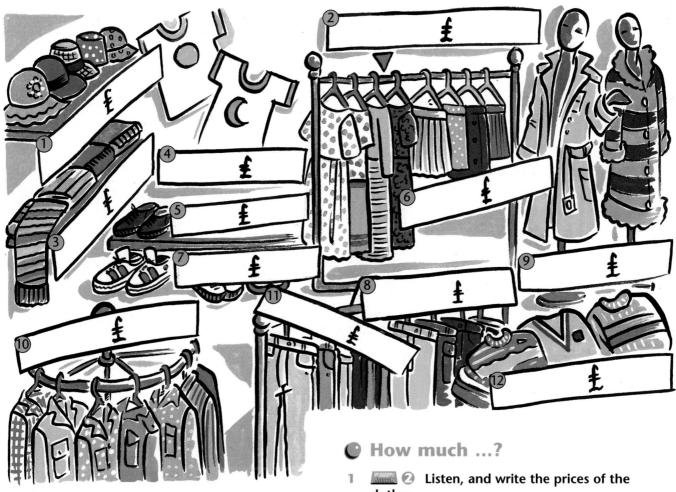

coats	jumpers	skirts	shoes
dresses	scarves	T-shirts	trainers
hats	shirts	jeans	trousers

● Clothes

1  ① **Listen, repeat and point.**

2 **Label the pictures.**

> **Look!**
>
> | | |
> |---|---|
> | a dress | a pair of jeans |
> | a T-shirt | a pair of shoes |

3 **What colour are the clothes? Ask and answer.**

What colour is the coat?
It's green / brown.
What colour are the jeans?
They're blue.

4 **What clothes have you got? Write a list. Ask your teacher for new words.**

a white T-shirt, a pair of blue trainers, ………

5 **Compare lists with a friend. Tell the class.**

I've got a white T-shirt. My friend has got a red T-shirt. We've both got a pair of blue trainers …

● How much …?

1  ❷ **Listen, and write the prices of the clothes.**

> **Look!**
>
> | | |
> |---|---|
> | 40p | 'forty p' |
> | £1.40 | 'one pound forty' |
> | £2.40 | 'two pounds forty' |
> | £1 = 100p | |

Pronunciation

2 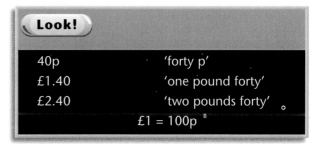 ❸ **Listen and read.**

Can I help you?
  How much are the red T-shirts?

They're £6 each.
  Can I have two, please?

That's £12.
  Here you are.

Thank you. Goodbye!
  Goodbye.

3 **Listen and repeat.**

4 **Underline the stressed words.**

5 **Act out the dialogue.**

6 **Make up dialogues for the other things in the shop.**

Ordinal numbers

1 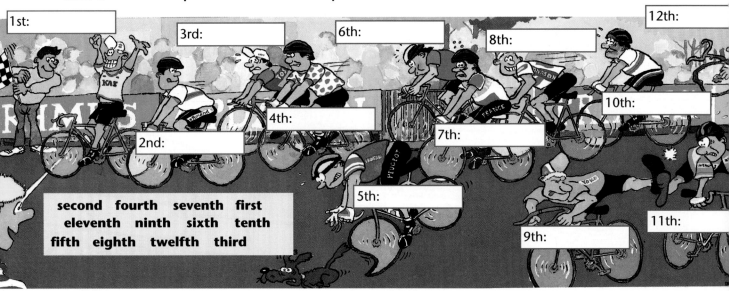 Listen and point. Then listen and repeat.   2 Write the correct word on each label.

1st:

3rd:

6th:

8th:

12th:

4th:

10th:

2nd:

7th:

5th:

11th:

9th:

second   fourth   seventh   first
eleventh   ninth   sixth   tenth
fifth   eighth   twelfth   third

Dates

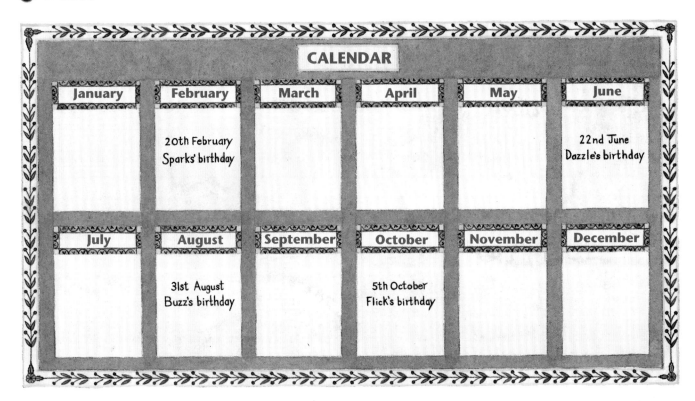

CALENDAR

| January | February | March | April | May | June |

20th February
Sparks' birthday

22nd June
Dazzle's birthday

| July | August | September | October | November | December |

31st August
Buzz's birthday

5th October
Flick's birthday

1  Listen and repeat the months.

2 When are their birthdays? Listen, point and repeat.

3 Add your birthday and your friend's birthday to the calendar.

When's your birthday?
It's the thirtieth of September.

4 Try and find a birthday for each month. Ask your friends and family and add their birthdays to your calendar.

Look!

| We write | It's 5th October. |
| We say | 'It's the fifth of October.' |

Do you like ...?

1 Match the words and pictures.

2 Tick (✔) the things you like. Cross (✗) the things you don't like.

3 Ask your friend. Add a tick (✔) or a cross (✗) for each thing.

Do you like football?
Yes, I do.
Do you like tennis?
No, I don't.

4 Tell the class.

I like tennis. My friend doesn't like tennis. We both like football.

	(✔ or ✗)	
	You	**Your friend**
☐ English		
☐ football		
☐ hamburgers		
☐ homework		
☐ ice cream		
☐ Maths		
☐ tennis		
☐ tests		

Think about it!

1 Label the clothes. Draw and label two more.

1 ....
2 ....
3 ....
4 ....
5 ....
6 ....

2 Write these ordinal numbers in words.

23rd ....

9th ....

2nd ....

48th ....

80th ....

3 a When's your birthday? Complete the sentence.

My birthday is ....

b When's your friend's birthday?

....

....

4 Complete the dialogue.

How much ...... the pens?

.... 90p each.

Can I .... two, please?

OK. That's £........., please.

Here you ....

Thank you. Goodbye.

Choose and circle.

Easy   OK   Difficult

Iceman!

can / can't

1 🎙 ① Listen and point.

2 Listen and repeat. Number the verbs.

Verbs

dance	☐	see	☐
draw	☐	sing	☐
hear	☐	speak	☐
read	☐	walk	☑ 1
run	☐	write	☐

3 Make sentences about the pictures. Use *he/she/they can/can't …*

1	*She can't see.*	5	....
2	....	6	....
3	....	7	....
4	....	8	....

4 Point to the pictures in Exercise 3. Ask and answer.

Can she see?
No, she can't.
Can they dance?
Yes, they can.

5 Ask your teacher for new verbs. Then ask and answer with your friend.

ride a motorbike   ski   ride a horse

cook   play the piano   drive a car

Can you cook?
Yes, I can.
Can you drive a car?
No, I can't.

6 Tell the class about your friend.

My friend can cook but he/she can't drive a car.

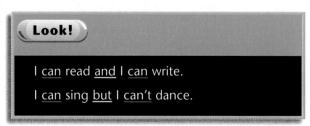

Look!

I can read and I can write.

I can sing but I can't dance.

Escape from Iceman!

1 Look at these six verbs. Choose three. You can do these three things but you can't do the other three things.

swim   ride a horse   climb

jump   drive a car   ride a motorbike

2 Listen and read.

> 1, 2, 3. 'Get over the wall. Climb or jump.' Oh no! I can't climb or jump. I don't throw again.

> 5! 1, 2, 3, 4, 5. 'Cross the river. Swim or ride a horse.' Great! I can swim. I throw again. 4!

3 Now play the game.

Don't!

1 **You are the teacher! Look and say.**

Don't write on the wall!
Don't eat in the classroom!

2 **Write rules for your classroom.**

RULES

DO	DON'T
Listen to the teacher.	Don't write on the walls.
...	...

Think about it!

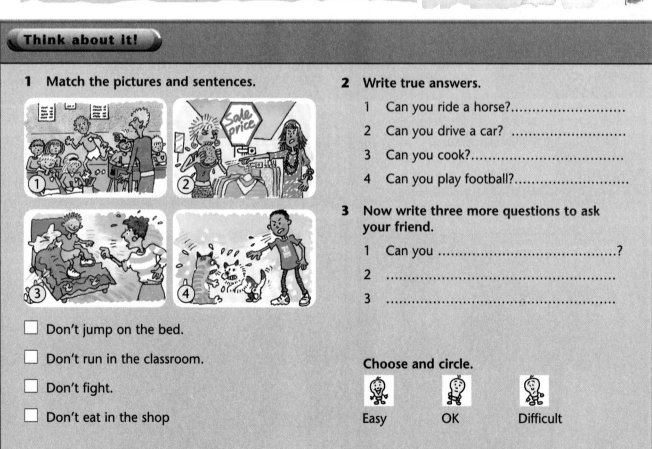

1 **Match the pictures and sentences.**

☐ Don't jump on the bed.

☐ Don't run in the classroom.

☐ Don't fight.

☐ Don't eat in the shop

2 **Write true answers.**

1 Can you ride a horse?..........................

2 Can you drive a car? ....

3 Can you cook?..................................

4 Can you play football?.........................

3 **Now write three more questions to ask your friend.**

1 Can you ....?

2 ....

3 ....

Choose and circle.

Easy   OK   Difficult

Fast food

1 **Look at the menu. How many words do you know?**

2 🎞 ❶ **Listen and repeat. Point to each thing in the pictures.**

3 **Describe each 'meal deal'.**

Meal 1 is a hamburger and fries, a salad and a Coke.

4 **Ask and answer about prices.**

How much is a cheeseburger?
It's £2.30.
How much is meal 2?
It's £3.95

Quick Bites Fast Food Restaurant

Meal deals!

1 £3.95

2 £3.95

3 £3.50

Menu

hamburger	£2.00
cheeseburger	£2.30
hot dog	£1.80
chicken nuggets	£2.50
Coke	90p
fruit juice	95p
milkshake	£1.10
mineral water	80p
fries	80p
salad	£1.20
apple pie	£1.60
ice cream	£1.50
doughnut	70p
tea	40p
coffee	50p

Meal deals!

4 £3.95

5 £1.95

6 £0.95p

5 🎞 ❷ **Listen and repeat the dialogue. Then practise it with a friend.**

Can I help you?
Yes. Can I have a hamburger and fries, please?
Here you are. Anything else?
Yes, a milkshake.
So, a hamburger and fries, and a milkshake. Let's see … that's £3.90 altogether, please.

6 **Make up more dialogues.**

Look!

fries *or*
French fries   =   chips

Are there any apples?

tomatoes   cheese   milk

rice

bread

water   oranges   fruit   bananas

sandwiches   apples

1 ⬛ ❸ Listen and point.

2 Listen and repeat. Write the words in the correct box.

There is some ...	There are some ...
cheese	apples
rice	tomatoes

3 Find more food and drink words on page 45. Add them to the boxes.

4 Look at the picture for one minute. Then close your book and answer the questions.
Is/Are there any ...?
Yes, there is/are.
No, there isn't/aren't.

Look!

There is some cheese.
There are some oranges.

There isn't any cheese.
There aren't any oranges.

Is there any cheese?
Are there any oranges?

Spot the difference

1 Work with a friend. One of you looks at picture ⓐ and the other looks at picture ⓑ.

2 Ask and answer. Can you find six differences?
Are there any ...?
Yes, there are./No, there aren't.
How many ... are there?
There are ...
What colour is/are ...?
It's/They're ...

a

q

Do you like …?

1  Listen to Buzz and Flick.

a) What food does Buzz like?

He likes apples.
He likes …

b) What food doesn't he like?

He doesn't like …

2 What about you? Make four lists. Ask you teacher for words you need.

Mmmm! I love …

I like …

I don't like …

Yuk! I hate …

3 Ask and answer with a friend.

Do you like cheese?

Yes, I do.

No, I don't.

Yes, I love it!

No, I hate it!

Think about it!

1 What's on the table? Write sentences.

There are some …*eggs*… and some ……………
There's some …………, a …………… and an
……………

2 Complete the dialogue.

Kim	I'm hungry. Have you got …… food?
Flick	Yes. I've got ………… apples.
Kim	Hmm. I ………… like apples. What about bread?
Flick	No, sorry. I haven't got …… bread.

3 Write sentences. Use *likes* and *doesn't like*.

Flick likes …………………………
She doesn't like …………………

Sparks ……………………………
He ………………………………

Choose and circle.

Easy OK Difficult

Revision

Units 6-10

Stop and think!

- Do the exercises on pages 48–51.
  Start with 'Dates and times'.
- Look at the HELP screens if you
  need more practice.

A Dates and times	OK	HELP
B *can/can't*	OK	HELP
C The verb *have got*	OK	HELP
D Food and drink	OK	HELP
E Shopping	OK	HELP

- Colour each letter when you
  can do the section.

(A (B (C (D (E)

Well done!

A

- Read and listen to 'The Backward Clock' on
  page 31 of the Student's Book.
- Look at page 38 of the Student's Book.
- Do Buzz words in Unit 8 of the Workbook.

B

- Look at page 41 of the Student's Book.
- Do Exercises 2 and 3 in Unit 9 of the
  Workbook.
- Read item 9 of the Grammar Summary.

C

- Look at page 29 of the Student's Book.
- Do Exercises 2–5 in Unit 6 of the Workbook.
- Read item 6 of the Grammar Summary.

D

- Look at page 45 of the Student's Book.
- Look at the 'Food and drink' pages in your
  vocabulary book.
- Do Buzz words in Unit 10 of the Workbook.

E

- Look at page 37 of the Student's Book.
- Do Exercises 8 and 9 in Unit 8 of the
  Workbook.
- Read item 10 of the Grammar Summary.

Dates and times

1 **Look at the tickets and find the dates. Then
complete the sentences.**

1 The flight to Istanbul is *on 14th September.*

2 The England–Chile football match is ....

  ....

3 'Hamlet' is ....

  ....

4 The Gloria Estefan concert is ....

  ....

5 The boat to Dublin is ....

  ....

2 📼 **❶ Listen. Fill in the times of the trains.**

Birmingham New Street		
Platform	Destination	Time
3	Liverpool	7.30
5	London	
1	Manchester	
8	Leeds	
14	Edinburgh	
9	Cardiff	

Look!

<u>at</u> two o'clock

<u>on</u> 14th October

⬤ can/can't

1 **Look at the chart. Say what Buzz and Dazzle can and can't do.**

Dazzle can play the recorder but Buzz can't.

2 **What can and can't *you* do? Put ticks and crosses in the other column.**

can (✔) can't (✘)	Buzz	Dazzle	You
play the recorder	✘	✔	
speak French	✔	✘	
ride a horse	✘	✘	
cook	✔	✘	
ride a bike	✘	✔	
swim	✔	✔	

3 **Answer the questions.**

1 Can Dazzle play the recorder?

Yes, she can.

2 Can Buzz play the recorder?

3 Can you play the recorder?

4 Can Dazzle speak French?

5 Can Buzz ride a horse?

6 Can Buzz cook?

7 Can you cook?

8 Can Dazzle ride a bike?

9 Can you ride a bike?

10 Can Buzz and Dazzle swim?

⬤ The verb *have got*

1 **Look at the table. Complete the short forms.**

short form	long form
I've got	I have got
you....... got	you have got
he....... got	he has got
she....... got	she has got
it....... got	it has got
we....... got	we have got
you....... got	you have got
they....... got	they have got

2 **Look at this question and answer. What do you notice about the order of the pronoun and verb?**

Has she got any brothers? *Yes, she has.*

3 **Write these negative forms in full.**

1 I haven't got any sweets.

I have not got any sweets.

2 You haven't got a computer.

3 He hasn't got a swimming pool.

4 We haven't got a mirror.

5 She hasn't got a whistle.

6 They haven't got any books.

4 📼 **❷ Listen. Complete and match the labels.**

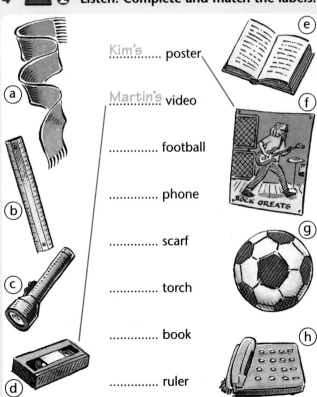

Kim's....... poster

Martin's.......... video

.... football

.... phone

.... scarf

.... torch

.... book

.... ruler

49

🔴 Food and drink

1 Complete these sentences with the correct word, 'some', 'any', 'a' or 'an'.

2 Look at the picture and write 'true' or 'false' for each sentence.

1 There are ..some.. eggs.   ..true..
2 There is .... orange.   ....
3 There isn't .... chocolate.   ....
4 There isn't .... cheese.   ....
5 There are .... apples.   ....
6 There aren't .... bananas.   ....
7 There is .... milk.   ....
8 There are .... tomatoes.   ....
9 There is .... bottle of water.   ....
10 There is .... rice.   ....

3 What do you like? Write sentences with 'like', 'don't like', 'love' or 'hate'.

1 (eggs)   ....
2 (oranges)   ....
3 (chocolate)   ....
4 (cheese)   ....
5 (apples)   ....
6 (bananas)   ....
7 (milk)   ....
8 (tomatoes)   ....

🔴 Shopping

1 Look at the shopping list and the picture. Ask and answer about the prices.

How much are apples?
They're 90p a kilo.

shopping list
2 kg apples
6 oranges
1 kg bananas
3 litres water
1 litre milk
4 apple pies

80p a kg
90p a kg
20p each
55p a litre
70p a litre
only £1·40 for 4

2 You've only got £3. What can you buy from the shopping list?

You can buy 2 kilos of apples and 6 oranges.
You can buy 1 kilo of apples, 4 oranges and ......

● Reading and writing

1 Match the ingredients with pictures 1–8.

INGREDIENTS

flour ☑ 4
butter ☐
water ☐
olive oil ☐
tomato ☐
onion ☐
cheese ☐
salt and pepper ☐

2 Read the recipe for pizza. Number the pictures in the correct order.

RECIPE

1 First, mix the flour and the butter together.
2 Then, add some water and a little olive oil.
3 Make the dough into a circle.
4 Next, cook the onion and tomato in some olive oil.
5 Add salt and pepper.
6 Spread the tomato and onion on to the circle of dough.
7 Put the cheese on top.
8 Finally, cook the pizza in the oven.

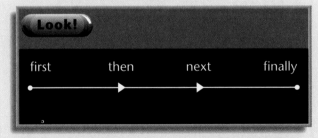

Look!

first   then   next   finally

3 Think of another easy recipe. Make a list of ingredients, then write the recipe.

● Project idea

● In groups, choose your favourite recipe.
● Write the list of ingredients and the recipe.
● Draw or find a picture.
● Display all the recipes on the wall or in a class recipe book.

New York

Mime

1 Listen and read.
2 Listen and repeat.

What's he doing?
No, he isn't.
Is he flying?
No, he isn't.
Is he swimming?
Yes, he is. Well done!

What are they doing?
Guess.
Are they singing?
No, they aren't.
Are they eating ice cream?
Yes, they are. Well done!

3 Choose an activity from the list. Mime it. Your friend guesses.

Are you writing a letter?
No, I'm not.
Are you drawing a picture?
Yes, I am.

Activities

read a book
dance
swim
fly
drink a cup of tea
drive a car
play tennis
draw a picture
wash the car
eat a hamburger
play football
listen to music
write a letter
sing

4 Now play in groups of three.

Is she dancing?
No, she isn't.
Is she playing football?
Yes, she is.

Look!

He is swimming.	He's swimming.
Is he swimming?	
They are eating.	They're eating.
Are they eating?	

Spelling

1 Look at the chart. Write the missing words.

eat		eating
play	+ ing	playing
draw		....
dance		dancing
drive	¢ + ing	driving
ride		....
stop		stopping
swim	double letter + ing	swimming
run		....

2 Test your spelling! Ask and answer with a friend about the words in the chart.

How do you spell 'eating'?
E-A-T-I-N-G

The streets of New York

1 Look at the pictures and read the sentences. Write the numbers.

a They're crossing the street. ....5....

b He's jogging. ......

c She's buying some nuts. ......

d He's playing the saxophone. ......

e He's reading a newspaper. ......

f He's riding a bike. ......

g She's roller-skating. ......

h They're looking in a shop window. ......

2 🎧 ❷ **Listen and check your answers.**

3 🎧 ❸ **Listen and read.**

4 **Listen and repeat.**

What are they doing?
They're crossing the street.
What's he doing?
He's jogging.

5 **Ask and answer about the other people in the pictures. Ask your teacher for words you need.**

6 Look at the people in pictures 1–6 and correct the sentences.

1 He's eating a sandwich.
He isn't eating a sandwich. He's …

2 She's reading a newspaper.
She isn't …

3 They're riding a bike.
They aren't …

4 She's looking in a shop window.

5 They're playing the saxophone.

6 He's riding a bike.

Look!

He isn't eating a sandwich.	They aren't riding a bike.
or	or
He's not eating a sandwich.	They're not riding a bike.

The streets of London

1 🎙️ ④ **Listen. Number the pictures.**

2 Write sentences.

A woman is eating a sandwich.

A man is playing the guitar.

3 Find pictures of people in a large city in *your* country. Write sentences about them.

Think about it!

1 What are they doing? Write sentences.

① ② ③ ④

1 She's ....

2 He ....

3 She ....

4 He ....

2 Complete the dialogue.

What .... you doing?

Guess!

Are you .... a sandwich?

No, I'm not.

.... reading a book?

No, I'm not.

.... a cup of tea?

Yes, I ......!

Choose and circle.

Easy   OK   Difficult

The escape

⬤ Where do you live?

1 🎧 **①** **Listen and read.**

1 Hi! My name's Rosana. I'm Brazilian. I'm 12 years old and I live in Rio de Janeiro.

2 Hello. I'm Ben and I'm 11. I'm British and I live in London with my mother and father. My grandfather is Indian. He lives in Bombay.

3 Hi! I'm Gizem. I'm 11 years old and I'm Turkish. I live in Ankara with my family. My aunt and uncle live in a small town near Pamukkale.

4 Hello. My name's Giovanni. I'm 10 years old and I live with my mother. We're Italian but we live in New York. I love New York!

5 Hi! I'm Emma. I'm British and I live in Manchester with my grandparents. I'm 12 years old.

> **Look!**
>
> I live in Rio.
> He live_s_ in Bombay
>
> We live in New York.
> They live near Pamukkale.

2 🎧 **②** **Listen and read.**

3 **Listen and repeat.**

Where does Rosana live?
She lives in Rio.
Where does Ben live?
He lives in London.

4 **Ask and answer about the other people.**

5 **Write five more questions. Can your friend answer them?**

How old is …?
What nationality is …?
What city/country/continent does …… live in?

> **Look!**
>
> Where <u>do</u> you live?
> Where <u>do</u> they live?
>
> Where <u>does</u> he live?
> Where <u>does</u> she live?

6 🎧 **③** **Listen to Rosie. Complete the first column of the chart.**

Name	Rosie	....
Age	....	....
Lives in:		
country	....	....
continent	....	....
Lives with	....	....
	....	....
	....	....

7 **Complete the second column of the chart with information about yourself.**

8 **Use your notes to write about yourself. Add a photo.**

My name's …

Countries and continents

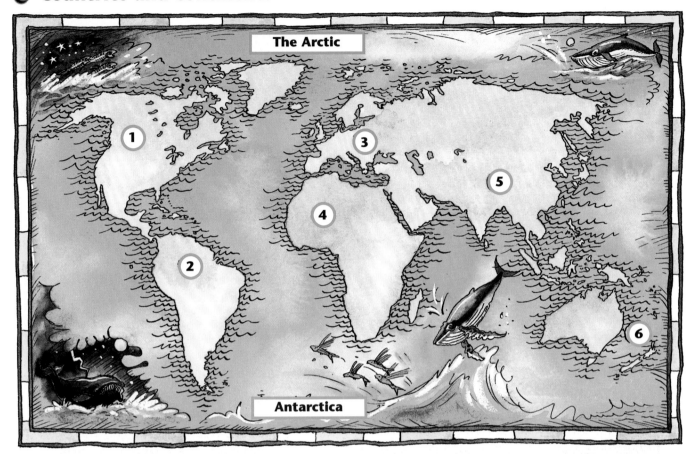

1 Look at the map. Label the continents.

Africa	North America
Europe	Australasia
Asia	South America

2 ⬛ ④ Listen and check your answers.

3 How many countries do you know in each continent? Ask your teacher for words you need.

Africa	Europe	Asia
Egypt	Portugal	India
....	....	....

North America	Australasia	South America
U.S.A.	Australia	Colombia
....	....	....

4 Match the countries and nationalities.

1 American   2 Argentinian   3 Australian

4 Brazilian   5 Hungarian   6 British

7 Irish   8 Polish   9 Spanish

10 Turkish   11 Greek   12 Portuguese

☐ America ☐ Hungary ☐ Portugal ☐ Brazil
☐ Poland ☐ Australia ☐ Argentina ☐ Turkey
☐ Greece ☐ Great Britain ☐ Ireland ☐ Spain

5 ⬛ ⑤ Listen and repeat the list of countries and nationalities.

6 Look at your list of countries from Exercise 3. Find out the nationalities. Ask your teacher or use a dictionary.

● Animals

1 Match the animals with their descriptions.

1 It's grey and very big! It lives in Africa. It eats plants. ....

2 It's very small. It lives in hot countries. It drinks blood. Yuk! ....

3 It's big and white. It lives in very cold countries. It eats fish. ....

4 It's brown, white and black. It lives in Asia. It eats other animals. ....

5 It lives in South America. It's a very long snake. It eats other animals. ....

polar bear

elephant

anaconda

tiger

mosquito

Think about it!

1 Complete the dialogue.

Hello. What's .... name?

....

How .... are you?

I'm .... years ....

What nationality .... you?

I'm ....

Where .... you ....?

I live in ....

2 Write three countries and their continents.

Country		Continent
....	is in	....
....	is in	....
....	is in	....

Choose and circle.

Easy   OK   Difficult

The rainforest

● Parts of the body

1 🎹 **①** **Listen and repeat the parts of the body.**

2 **Complete the labels.**

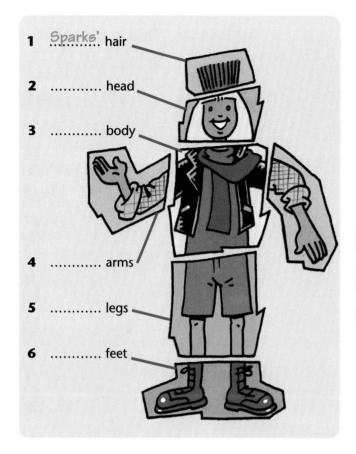

1 ....Sparks'...... hair

2 .... head

3 .... body

4 .... arms

5 .... legs

6 .... feet

3 🎹 **②** **Listen and match.**

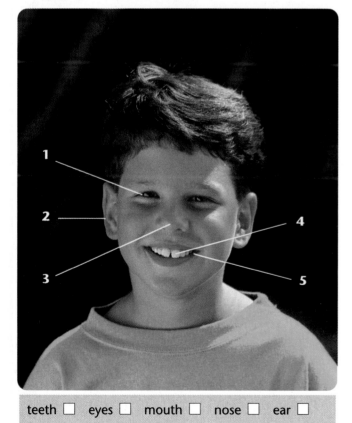

teeth ☐ eyes ☐ mouth ☐ nose ☐ ear ☐

4 🎹 **③** **Which person is it? Listen and tick (✔).**

1 a ☐ b ☐

2 a ☐ b ☐

3 a ☐ b ☐

4 a ☐ b ☐

5 **Find pictures of famous people. Describe them. Use these words.**

Colour of eyes	brown, green, blue, grey
Hair – colour	black, brown, fair, blonde
– style	long, short, curly, straight

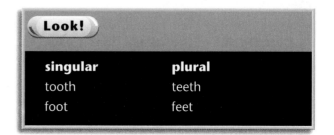

Look!

singular	plural
tooth	teeth
foot	feet

More animals!

1 Look at the animals. What noises do they make?
2 Listen and match. Write the numbers.

cat

parrot

elephant

alligator

dog

frog

monkey

bee

lion

mosquito

3 Listen, repeat and check your answers.
4 Make a list of words you need to talk about animals.

6 Find or draw a picture of another animal. Write a paragraph to describe it. Say where it lives and what it eats.

adjectives	parts of the body	colours	countries
brown	ears	long	Turkey

5 Describe one of the animals on this page. Your friend guesses.

It lives in Africa. It's very large. It's grey. It's got big ears and …
Is it an elephant?
Yes, it is!

These are wild horses. They live in New South Wales, in Australia. They eat grass.

Alligator, Alligator!

1 🎵 6 **Listen and read.**
2 **Say the chant.**

Alligator, alligator, in the Nile
Looking at me with a great big smile
What's it going to do? What's it going to do?
It's going to bite you!

Rattlesnake, rattlesnake, on the ground
Looking at me – Hey! What's that sound?
What's it going to do? What's it going to do?
It's going to bite you!

Bumble bee, bumble bee, in the air
Looking at me – now it's in my hair
What's it going to do? What's it going to do?
It's going to sting you!

Think about it!

1 Match the sentences and the pictures.

1 She's got curly, blonde hair and green eyes. ......
2 She's got long, blonde hair and blue eyes. ......
3 She's got straight, dark hair and brown eyes. ......
4 She's got short, dark hair and brown eyes. ......

2 Describe this boy.

....
....
....
....

3 Label the parts of the body. Use these words:

ear
head
arm
leg
foot

Choose and circle.

Easy   OK   Difficult

The end of Iceman

The days of the week

1  **Listen and read.**

Sneeze on Monday, sneeze for luck
Sneeze on Tuesday, meet a duck
Sneeze on Wednesday, see a bat
Sneeze on Thursday, find a cat
Sneeze on Friday, dance and shout
Sneeze on Saturday, school is out
Sneeze on Sunday morning, too
Now you've got a cold – aaaachoooo!

2 **Underline the days of the week. Now say them.**

3 **Match the days of the week with the pictures.**

4 **Say the poem.**

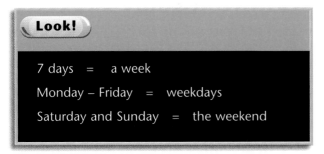

Look!

7 days	=	a week
Monday – Friday	=	weekdays
Saturday and Sunday	=	the weekend

going to …

Saturday

morning	buy some clothes
afternoon	play football
evening	watch a video

Sunday

morning	stay in bed!
afternoon	visit my grandparents
evening	do my homework

1 **Look at Martin's diary. What's he going to do at the weekend?**

On Saturday morning, he's going to buy some clothes.

On Saturday afternoon, he's going to …

Look!

He is going to …

Is he going to …?

2 **Write your own diary.**

Saturday

morning	
afternoon	
evening	

Sunday

morning	
afternoon	
evening	

3 **Guess what your friend is going to do.**

Are you going to watch television on Saturday morning?

Yes, I am. / No, I'm not.

4 **Ask other friends. Find people who are going to do the same things.**

Weather and seasons

1  ② Look, listen and read.
2 Listen and repeat.

1 it's rainy   2 it's cloudy   3 it's hot   4 it's cold

5 it's snowy   6 it's windy   7 it's dry   8 it's sunny

3 ③ Listen and repeat the names of the seasons.

4 Read about the seasons in London and Buenos Aires.
Write the missing words.

London in winter ➡

WINTER	December, ① ...., February : cold and ② ....
SPRING	March, ③ ...., May : mild, quite sunny
SUMMER	June, ④ ...., August : hot and dry
AUTUMN	September, ⑤ ...., November : mild, windy and rainy

Buenos Aires ⬅ in summer

June, ⑥ ...., August : quite ⑦ .... but not snowy	WINTER
September, ⑧ ...., November : mild, quite sunny	SPRING
December, ⑨ ...., February : very ⑩ .... and humid	SUMMER
March, ⑪ ...., May : mild, quite rainy	AUTUMN

5 Describe the seasons in your own country.
6 ④ Listen and number the pictures.

Summer holiday

1 **Look at the picture. Which country do you think this place is in?**

2 **Answer the questions. Ask your teacher for new words or look in a dictionary.**

> How many people are there?
>
> What are they doing?
>
> What are they going to do?
>
> What's the weather like?
>
> Can you see any animals?
>
> What are the people wearing?
>
> Do you like this place?

3 **Point to the people in the picture. Ask and answer.**

What's he doing?
He's playing football.
What's she wearing?
She's wearing a red T-shirt.

4 **Find a picture of a place in your country. Describe it. Use the questions in Exercise 2 to help you.**

Think about it!

1 **Look at Flick's diary. Write the missing days.**

Monday	buy a new pair of jeans
....	play football
....	watch television
Thursday	buy a present for Sparks
....	watch a video
....	play tennis
Sunday	write a letter

2 **Write what Flick is going to do on each day.**

- On Monday, she's going to ...

3 **Match the words and pictures.**

rainy ☐ sunny ☐ windy ☐ snowy ☐

① ② ③ ④

Choose and circle.

Easy   OK   Difficult

The storm

🌑 Back in the real world

1 **Kim and Martin are back in the real world. What do you think they do:**

 a on weekdays?
 b at weekends?

2 **Read the text quickly. Check your ideas from Exercise 1.**

3 📼 ❶ **Read and listen. Answer the questions.**

 1 What time does Kim go to school?
 2 What time does she leave school?
 3 Does she go to school on Saturday?
 4 Does she have a piano lesson on Saturday?

4 **Write more questions about Kim's week. Can your friend answer them?**

5 **Find more examples to add to this chart.**

> **Look!**
>
> She <u>has</u> a piano lesson.
> She <u>doesn't have</u> a piano lesson.
> <u>Does</u> she <u>have</u> a piano lesson?

in	on	at
in the morning	on Saturday	at half past eight
in the summer	on 15th April	at four o'clock
in September	on Sunday morning	at the weekend
....	....	....
....	....	....
....	....	....

Well, I'm back in the real world now. And my life is back to normal!
Tomorrow is Monday and I've got school.

I go to school at half past eight every morning on weekdays. I leave school at four o'clock in the afternoon. In the evening, I do my homework. Then I go to bed early.
I don't go to school at the weekend. I have dancing lessons on Saturday morning and a piano lesson in the afternoon. In the evening, I watch television.
Then, on Sunday, I sleep in the morning. In the afternoon, I go to the park with my friends. In the evening I listen to music.
I think Sunday is my favourite day!

My week

1 Read about Gizem's week. Complete her notes.

name   Gizem
live in:
    city   ....
    country   ....
start school at   8.00 a.m.
finish school at   ...... p.m.
weekday evenings   do ....
weekends:
    day   ...... shopping or play ....
    evening   watch .... or go to
    the ....

My name's Gizem and I live in Ankara, the capital of Turkey. On weekdays, I go to school from 8 o'clock in the morning until 4 o'clock in the afternoon. In the evening, I do my homework. I get a lot of homework!

At the weekend, I see my friends. During the day, we go shopping or play volleyball. I love volleyball! In the evening, we watch television or go to the cinema.

2 Who is this boy? Read about him on page 57. Then complete his notes.

name   ....
live in:
    city   ....
    country   England
start school at   8.30 a.m.
finish school at   4.00 p.m.
weekday evenings   do homework or watch
    television
weekends:
    day   go swimming or play football
    evenings   play computer games or
    watch videos

3 Now complete the paragraph about the boy.

My name's .... and I .... in ...., England. During the week, I .... school from 8.30 in the morning until ...... o'clock in the afternoon. In the evening, I .... my .... or ....
I .... go to school at the weekend. During the day, I go .... or ....
.... with my friends. In the evening, I play .... games or ....

Look!

| 8.00 a.m. | = | 8 o'clock in the morning |
| 4.00 p.m. | = | 4 o'clock in the afternoon |

4 Make notes about your own week.

5 Write a paragraph about your week.

play tennis   phone friends

go sailing

listen to music   read magazines

have a music lesson

1  ②
Listen and read.
2 Sing the song.

Livewires Song

Is it all real?
Or only in my mind?
Is it just a book?
Or is there something else behind?

Yes this is real
It isn't just pretend
This is our world
And now you are our friend.

Welcome to our world
We've got everything you need
Open your book and turn the page
We're in everything you read.

Welcome to our world
It's exciting and new

The Livewires are waiting for you!

Think about it!

1 **Complete the questions. Then write true answers about your week.**

1 Do you go ...... school ...... Saturday?

....

2 ...... time ...... you leave school?

....

3 What ...... you ...... on Sunday evening?

....

4 ...... Sunday your favourite ....?

....

2 **Write *in, at* or *on*.**

1 ...... Tuesday

2 ...... five o'clock

3 ...... the weekend

4 ...... the spring

5 ...... 23rd May

6 ...... the morning

Choose and circle.

Easy   OK   Difficult

Revision

Units 11-15

Stop and think!

- Do the exercises on pages 72–74. Start with 'Nationalities'.
- Look at the HELP screens if you need more practice.

A Nationalities	OK	HELP	
B *going to*	OK	HELP	
C Present continuous	OK	HELP	
D Present simple	OK	HELP	
E Weather map	OK	HELP	

- Colour each letter when you can do the section.

(A) (B) (C) (D) (E)

Well done!

A

- Look at page 58 of the Student's Book.
- Find more countries in an atlas or Geography book.
- Find the words for nationalities in a dictionary or encyclopaedia.

B

- Read and listen to the song 'Alligator, Alligator' on page 63.
- Do Exercises 2 and 4 in Unit 13 of the Workbook.
- Read item 13 of the Grammar Summary.

C

- Look at pages 54–5 of the Student's Book.
- Do Exercises 2–4 in Unit 11 of the Workbook.
- Read item 12 of the Grammar Summary.

D

- Look at page 69 of the Student's Book.
- Do Exercises 2 and 3 in Unit 15 of the Workbook.
- Read item 8 of the Grammar Summary.

E

- Look at page 66 of the Student's Book.
- Look at Think about it! in Unit 14 of the Student's Book.
- Do Buzz words in Unit 14 of the Workbook.

Nationalities

1 Write the nationalities. Add two more.

country	nationality	country	nationality
America	American	Hungary	
Argentina		Ireland	
Australia		Poland	
Brazil		Portugal	
China		Spain	
Great Britain		Turkey	
France			
Greece			

2 Copy these four headings into your notebook. Look at the endings of the nationalities and write them under the correct headings.

- an	- ish
American	

- ese	other

3 Find more nationalities. Add them to the boxes in Exercise 2.

● *going to*

1 Look at the table. Write a sentence in your notebook for each picture.

He			sing.
	is		mend the car.
She		going to	play football.
			eat a sandwich.
They	are		write a letter.
			play the recorder.

2 Now write sentences for these pictures.

● Present continuous

1 Look at the picture and read the text. Write the names.

1	5	9 ....
2	6	10 ....
3	7	11 ....
4 *Sam*	8	12 ....

There are lots of people in the park. Sam and Carl are playing football. Sam is wearing a scarf. Sam's sister, Gina, is playing football, too. Paula and Tessa are both singing, but Paula isn't playing the guitar. Sue and her sister, Emily, are roller-skating. Emily is listening to music. Their brother, Tom, is eating an ice cream. Jerry and Martin are riding their bikes. Martin is wearing a blue T-shirt. Jake and Andy are reading. Andy is eating a sandwich.

2 Look at the picture again and complete these sentences.

1 Carl is *wearing* a *grey* T-shirt.
2 Paula is .... the tambourine.
3 Emily .... a sandwich.
4 Jerry is wearing a .... T-shirt.
5 Andy .... eating an ice cream.
6 Sue .... listening to music.

Present simple

1 **Complete these questions and answers with *do*, *does*, *don't* or *doesn't*.**

1 .... you live in England?

No, I ....

2 .... Martin go to school?

Yes, he ....

3 .... Martin's friends like football?

Yes, they ....

4 .... your sisters have piano lessons?

No, they ....

5 .... you both like ketchup?

Yes, we ....

6 .... you remember her name?

No, I ....

2 **Read what these people say. Then write descriptions in your notebook.**

1 Hi! My name's Sally. I live in London. I like music and sport – and I love food!

Sally lives in London. She likes music and sport. She loves food.

2 I'm Julian. I live in Manchester. I have piano lessons every Saturday, but I hate music.

3 Hello, I'm Kate. I live in Glasgow, in Scotland. I watch TV every evening, and I talk to my friends on the telephone.

4 I'm Harry. I live in Oxford. I have lunch at school every day. I love hamburgers and chips.

5 Hello, I'm Rachel. I go jogging every morning. I love exercise – and I hate fast food!

6 My name's Dan. I live in Belfast. I play football every evening after school. At weekends, I watch TV or go out with my friends.

3 **Write about two friends or family members. Write paragraphs like the ones in Exercise 2.**

Weather map

1 **Look at the map and complete the text. Use these words.**

cloudy   rainy   snowy   sunny   windy

This map shows what the weather is like in Europe today. In England, it is (1).............. and cold. In Scotland it is (2)............. But in Turkey, the weather is good. In fact, in Ankara it is hot and (3) .... In Italy, it is (4) .... In Ireland it is (5) .... and cold.

2 **What is the weather like where you are now?**

Reading and writing

1 Read about Juliet's favourite animal.

My favourite animal is a panda. It lives in China. A panda is a large, black and white animal. It eats bamboo. There are only about 5,000 pandas in the world today.

2 Answer these questions about the panda.

1 Where does it live?

2 Is it large or small?

3 What colour is it?

4 What does it eat?

5 How many are there in the world?

3 Choose two of these animals and write a short paragraph about each of them. (Use the questions in Exercise 2 to make notes first.)

gorilla

dolphin

tiger

rhino

spider

eagle

Project idea

● As a class, draw a large map of the world.

● Find or draw pictures of your favourite animals. In groups, write short texts about the animals.

● Put the pictures and texts on the map to show where the animals live.

Grammar Summary

1 be

a statements

+	
short forms	**full forms**
I'm	I am
you're	you are
he she 's it	he she is it
we you 're they	we you are they

There is no short form of *this is*.

⊖	
short forms	**full forms**
I'm not	I am not
you aren't	you are not
he she isn't it	he she is not it
we you aren't they	we you are not they

There is another short form of the negative.

*you're not   she's not   he's not   it's not
we're not   they're not*

b questions and short answers

Short answers begin with *Yes* or *No*.

Is she your friend?   *Yes, she is.
No, she isn't.
or No, she's not.*

Are they friends?   *Yes, they are.
No, they aren't.
or No, they're not.*

c question words

A lot of question words begin with *Wh-*. The answers
don't begin with *Yes* or *No*.

What's this?   *It's a book.*
Where's Buzz?   *He's in the shed.*
Who's Dazzle?   *She's my friend.*
How are you?   *I'm fine, thank you.*

2 there is / there are

a statements

+	
short form	**full forms**
there's	there is
—	there are

⊖	
short forms	**full forms**
there isn't	there is not
there aren't	there are not

There is no short form of *there are*.

b questions and answers

Is there a pen in your bag?
    Yes, there is.
    No, there isn't.
Are there any books on the table?
    Yes, there are.
    No, there aren't.
How many pencils are there?
    There are seven.

3 a/an

We normally use *an* if the word begins with a
vowel (a, e, i, o, u). We normally use *a* if the word
begins with a consonant.

an aeroplane
an orange

a book
a pencil

4 imperatives

Be quiet.   *Don't talk.*
Open the window.   *Don't open the window.*

5 plurals

To make most plurals, we add -s or -es.

books	videos
boxes	tomatoes

Some plurals are irregular.

man	men
woman	women
child	children
tooth	teeth
foot	feet

We normally use *people* as the plural of *person*.

6 have got/has got

a statements

The short forms of *have got* and *has got* are *-'ve got* and *-'s got*.

I've got a bicycle.
She's got a bicycle.

The negative forms of *have got* and *has got* are *haven't got* and *hasn't got*.

I haven't got a tennis racket.
He hasn't got a tennis racket.

b questions and short answers

Has he got a whistle?	*Yes, he has.*
	No, he hasn't.
Have they got a swimming pool?	*Yes, they have.*
	No, they haven't.

7 genitives

We use *'s* to show possession. We can use it with names and with people or animals.

Dazzle's mirror
the dog's toy

With plurals ending in -s, we just add an apostrophe (').

the girls' bedroom	*(two or more girls)*
the girl's bedroom	*(one girl)*

We normally do the same if a name ends in -s.

Sparks' house

8 present simple

a statements

Only the third person singular (he / she / it) form is different. It has -s or -es on the end.

I/you/we/they want/go...
he/she wants/goes...

b questions

To make questions we put *do* or *does* in front of the subject (I, you, he, etc). We do not add -s to the verb in the third person singular.

Do you want.......?	*Yes you do.*
Does she want....?	*No you don't.*

We can put question words in front of *do* or *does*.

What does he want for his birthday?
  He wants a bike.
Where does he live?
  He lives in Turkey.

9 can/can't

a statements

I can swim	*I can't swim.*
We can swim	*We can't swim.*

The full form of *can't* is *cannot*.

b questions and short answers

Can he ride a bike?	*Yes, he can.*
Can they ride a bike?	*No they can't.*

10 some/any

a some

We sometimes use numbers with plural nouns.

There are five boxes in the cupboard.
There are ten people in the garden.

We use *some* when we don't know the exact number or when it isn't important.

There are some boxes in the cupboard.
There are some people in the garden.

b some with singular nouns

We use *some* with certain singular nouns. Often, these nouns do not have a plural form.

There is some bread in the cupboard.
There is some money on the table.

c any with singular and plural nouns

We normally use *any* instead of *some* in questions and negative statements.

Are there any boxes in the cupboard?
There aren't any people in the garden.
Is there any bread in the cupboard?
There isn't any money on the table.

But we often use *some* with *Do you want ...?* and *Can I have ...?*

Do you want some cheese?
Can I have some water?

11 *How much/many ...?*

We use *How much ...?* with singular nouns.

How much bread is there?
How much money have you got?

We use *How many ...?* with plural nouns.
The answer is often a number.

How many people are there?
There are ten.

12 present continuous

a statements

You make the present continuous tense with *be* and the *-ing* form of the verb.

He's playing.   *They're playing.*

There are two short forms in the negative (except for the first person singular). Both are correct.

They're not listening.   *They aren't listening.*

b questions and answers

The short answers are the same as the short answer for *be*.

Is she playing?   *Yes, she is.*
Are you playing?   *No, you aren't.*

We can also make questions by adding a question word at the beginning.

What are you playing?
I'm playing football.

Who are you playing football with?
I'm playing football with my friends.

c *-ing* forms: spelling

Use this table to help you spell *-ing* forms.

verb	spelling	*-ing* form
eat play draw	+ ing	eating playing drawing
dance drive ride	e̶ + ing	dancing driving riding
stop swim run	double letter + ing	stopping swimming running

13 *going to*

We can use *going to* to talk about the future.

I'm going to phone my cousin tomorrow.

We make statements, questions and answers in the same way as we do for the present continuous. Study the examples:

He's not going to phone his aunt. or *He isn't going to phone his aunt.*

Are you going to practise the piano?
Yes, I am. / No, I'm not.

What are you going to have for dinner?

14 time: *on/at/in*

We use *on* for:

● days of the week   *on Wednesday*
● dates   *on 21st March*

We use *at* for:

● times of day   *at four o'clock*
● *at night*
● *at the weekend*

We use *in* for:

● parts of the day   *in the morning / afternoon*
● months   *in April*
● seasons   *in the summer*

Oxford University Press
Great Clarendon Street
Oxford OX2 6DP

Oxford New York Athens Auckland Bangkok
Bogota Bombay Buenos Aires Calcutta Cape Town
Dar es Salaam Delhi Florence Hong Kong Istanbul
Karachi Kuala Lumpur Madras Madrid Melbourne
Mexico City Nairobi Paris Singapore Taipei Tokyo
Toronto Warsaw

and associated companies in
Berlin Ibadan

OXFORD and OXFORD ENGLISH
are trade marks of Oxford University Press

ISBN 0 19 4356965

© Oxford University Press 1998

Printed in Spain

Acknowledgements

Illustrations by:

Katherine Baxter pp 41, 53, 70. Brett Breckon pp 6, 31, 42,
50, 51, 63, 67. Michael Brownlow pp 4, 7, 8, 9, 11, 12, 13,
15, 16, 19,20, 21, 22, 28, 29, 32, 33, 36, 40, 44, 47, 52, 56,
60, 61, 64, 67, 68, 71. Sally Chambers pp 17, 30, 33.
Phil Dobson pp 17, 41. David Eaton p 46. Kevin Faerber
pp 34, 53. Roger Fereday pp 15, 19, 41, 43, 73. Peter Joyce
pp 42, 43, 73. Sarah Jowsey pp 38, 45, 46, 50, 66.
Barry Rowe p 39. Francis Scappaticci pp 10, 21, 25, 26, 37,
61, 63. Tim Slade pp 5, 7, 10, 11, 15, 21, 23, 25, 26, 27, 31,
35, 39, 47, 48, 49, 55, 67. Martin Ursell pp 18, 24, 58, 74.
Bart Verney pp 15, 26, 27, 38, 65.

Location Photography:

Julie Fisher

**The publishers would like to thank the following
organizations for their help & co-operation:**

Artists Collective Theatre School
Drayton Manor High School
Freda Gill

**The publishers would like to thank the following for their
permission to reproduce photographs & other copyright
material:**

Heather Angel/Biofotos pp 62 (Scarlet Macaw), 75 (Tiger).
Ardea London Ltd. pp 59 (Polar Bear, Siberian Tiger,
Mosquito, Snake), 62 (Monkey, Bumblebee, Alligator,
Mosquito, Cat, Cocker Spaniel, Lion, Frog, Horses).
Bruce Coleman Ltd. pp 59 (Elephant), 75 (Gorilla, Dolphin,
Rhinoceros, Tarantula). Collections pp 55 (Nigel French/
Changing of The Guard, Liba Taylor/Portobello Market, Geoff
Howard/Selling Chestnuts, Brian Shuel/Hyde Park, Liba
Taylor/Lady with deckchairs), 57 (Sandra Lousada/ Brazilian
Girl). Colorific p 54 (John Goldblatt/Stall, New York) James
Davis Travel Photography p 66 (Buenos Aires).
Eye Ubiquitous pp 54 (Bruce Adams/6th Avenue N.Y.C. Suki
Coe/New York), 55 (Paul Thompson/Commuters).
Pictor International Ltd. pp 25 (Old Man, Karl, Carol, Sam),
55 (Lorry), 57 (Houses of Parliament, Turkish Girl,
Manchester, Polish girl), 61 (12 year old girl), 70 (Turkish
Girl), 74 (Sally, Julian, Rachel). Tony Stone Images pp 25
(Peter Correz/Old Woman, Ken Fisher/Michael, Bob
Thomas/Sally, Peter Correz/David, Dan Bosler/Lucy, Ken
Fisher/Mark), 54 (Will & Deni Mcintyre/Fifth Avenue,
Teenagers Roller-blading, Chris Cheadle/Runner on Brooklyn
Bridge), 55 (Timothy Shonnard/Executives eating), 57 (Tony
Latham/Asian Boy, David C Tomlinson/Pamukkale, Turkey,
Jon Ortner/New York Skyline, Jerome Tisne/11 year old boy,
Kevin Morris/Teenage Girl) 63 (David Madison/Jogger) 66
(Ambrose Greenway/Hyde Park), 70 (Tony Latham/Asian
Boy), 74 (Tony Latham/Kate, Don Smetzer/Harry, Ken
Fisher/Dan). Telegraph Colour Library pp 54 (John
Heseltine/New York, Francesca Yorke/Bryant Park, New
York), 55 (Covent Garden). B & M Totterdell Photography
p 70 (Volley-Ball)